THE POWER OF
ATTITUDE

Featuring the Story of George Washington

Author
Patricia Metten

Art Illustrator
Stephen P. Krause

Editor, Layout and Research
Beatrice W. Friel

THE POWER OF
ATTITUDE

Featuring the Story of George Washington

Advisors
Paul and Millie Cheesman
Mark Ray Davis
Rodney L. Mann, Jr.
Roxanne Shallenberger
Dale T. Tingey

Publisher
Steven R. Shallenberger

Director and Correlator
Lael J. Woodbury

AN EAGLE SYSTEMS
INTERNATIONAL
PUBLICATION

ANTIOCH, CALIFORNIA

The Power of Attitude
Copyright © 1981 by
Power Tales
Eagle Systems International
P.O. Box 1229
Antioch, California 94509

ISBN: 0-911712-91-7

Library of Congress Catalog No.: 81-50865

First Edition

Lithographed in USA by
COMMUNITY PRESS, INC.

A member of
The American Bookseller's Association
New York, New York

Dedicated to children everywhere with the hope they will realize that their attitude will influence their achievements.

GEORGE WASHINGTON

George Washington was born in February 1732 in Westmoreland County, Virginia, the eldest of four sons and two daughters of Augustine and Mary Ball Washington. He also had two older half brothers. His father was a well-to-do planter. His mother was a woman of ability and character, who gave her children good training.

George grew up as a plantation owner's son. Until he was eleven, he received his education from his father. After his father died, George spent most of his time with his half brother Lawrence. It was while living with Lawrence that George became interested in surveying, and in 1749 he was appointed surveyor of Culpeper County.

It was also through Lawrence that George became involved in the Virginia militia. In 1752, while holding the rank of major, George was appointed adjutant-general in charge over one of the four military districts in the state of Virginia. In the winter of 1753 he undertook a wilderness journey of 1,000 miles to warn the French not to trespass on British territory.

George served as an officer in the militia until 1758, when the French were no longer a threat to Virginia. On 6 January 1759 he married Martha Dandridge Custis, a widow with a son and daughter by a previous marriage. Although George and Martha had no children of their own, he helped Martha raise her two children as if they were his own. Later, when Martha's son and his wife died, George and Martha adopted their children.

As disputes with Great Britain grew more bitter, a Continental Congress was formed and George was chosen as a delegate. On 15 June 1775 he was unanimously elected commander-in-chief of the Continental Army. Because his men were untrained and ill-equippped, they suffered many defeats. However, George continued to persevere and, with the aid of the French, the war ended in the surrender of Lord Cornwallis.

With the signing of the peace treaty in 1783, George resigned and returned to civilian life at Mount Vernon. However, his retirement didn't last long, for in 1787 he was the unanimous choice to preside at the convention that produced the Constitution of the United States.

In February of 1789, at the age of fifty-seven, George was unanimously elected the first President of the United States. He served for two terms, eight years total, during which time he established the country's finances, industry, commerce, and agriculture on a firm basis. Under his leadership the young republic earned the respect of the world. Declining the nomination for a third term, George again retired to Mount Vernon and private life.

One cold, snowy day in December, after George had returned from a long horseback ride around his plantation, he discovered his throat was sore. During the night it became extremely difficult for him to breathe. The next day, 14 December 1799, George died at the age of sixty-seven.

Welcome to my story! I am Baldy Eagle, and you may already know that I am the official emblem for the United States of America. From my viewpoint high in the sky I've been able to watch this country grow from a tiny colony to a strong, big nation. There have been certain people along the way who have been great leaders for America, and I'm going to tell you about one of them.

Would you like to guess who this story is about? Here is a clue: "First in war, first in peace, and first in the hearts of his countrymen." Or maybe you know him better as the father of our country. Hold on, because we're

about to enter the life and times of George Washington, first President of the United States of America!

Yes sir, Baldy Eagle was watching when little George wrote his first lessons on a homemade notebook. I saw him riding through the mountains and woods marking out farms and making maps. I even watched him writing in his diaries and sending messages during the Revolutionary War. You may wonder how I could do that. Well, I'll tell you. Eagles have very fine eyesight, and we can see tiny details on the ground while we're flying

high in the sky. In fact, people who can see very small things are said to have an "eagle eye."

So when I tell you about what George did, you can believe me. There hasn't been much that old Baldy Eagle has missed while this country was growing up!

Often I heard George say to his mother, "If you don't need me right now, I'm going out in the woods." That boy did love being out in nature. He was born in Virginia in 1732, and by the time he was seven he was living on a large farm, called a plantation, near the Rappahannock River. He had to work very hard on this farm, but he learned to enjoy it because he had the right attitude. Instead of wishing he could be doing something else more fun, George did his work carefully and tried to pay close attention so he could learn something.

When George was eleven, his father died, and from then on George had to help manage the plantation. Although he only went to school until he was about fifteen, George learned to write well, keep good records of how he spent his money, and do simple arithmetic.

Many times I would be flying over the woods and valleys by the Rappahannock River, and I'd see George out riding his horse. Sometimes he'd get off his horse and kneel down on the ground, scooping up a handful of dirt. One day I heard him talking softly to himself, kind of

14

thinking out loud. He was just standing by his horse looking at the land, saying, "I guess there's not a prettier place on this whole earth than the land of Virginia. From this hill I can see for miles and miles. There must be forests and mountains clear to the end of the world."

Then he picked some of the wildflowers growing 'round him and took a whiff. "Smelling the flowers and the magnolia trees makes me feel happy all over," he said. "Why, I could ride for days and never see another human being. I'd feel nothing but sunlight coming through the trees warming my back, and maybe I'd see panther tracks in the soft brown earth. This must be the best place on God's earth."

16

Then George climbed back on his horse and rode slowly through the woods. He was enjoying the sights and sounds too much to hurry.

Another time I saw George sitting on his horse at the top of a high hill. They were just standing there quiet-like, and George said, looking toward the West, "I'm coming your direction one of these days." Then I knew that

he wasn't going to stay in Virginia, even though he loved it. One thing for sure, George was a man on the go.

As things turned out, only a few months later George found himself on a month-long expedition through the very wilderness he loved. He could have stayed home enjoying the comforts of plantation life, but his attitude toward learning led him to seek new opportunities. He did so well on the trip that he was made an assistant to the man in charge of exploring land beyond Virginia.

Being an assistant was a great opportunity for George. He learned to draw maps, survey land, and establish boundaries. In fact, by the time he was eighteen he was earning all his own money by working as a surveyor. He also started buying land for himself just about that time.

When he was twenty, George became interested in military affairs. He joined the army and worked hard at being a good soldier. He always tried to do his best at whatever he was doing. I heard him tell someone once, "If I can't be improved as a person after I've done something, I've wasted my time doing it."

While George was in the military, the British and the French were about to fight each other over the Ohio River Valley. The British wanted the land so their people could start farming it. The French were more interested in having it because it was rich with animals, and the French wanted to sell the animals' fur.

The British decided to send an important message to the French in the Ohio River Valley. It would be a dangerous journey for the messenger because it was winter and the temperatures were freezing. I heard George talking it over with a friend.

"You know, Jeff," George was saying, "I don't have to be the one who takes the message. I am mighty tempted to let someone else do it." His friend poked a stick in the fire and answered, "Whoever takes this message will have to sleep out in the wilderness and find his own food. There will be wild animals—bears and wolves, maybe Indians, too. And crossing those rivers isn't going to be easy either."

George looked around the comfortable front room of the plantation house. He could hear the wind howling outside, but it was warm and dry and safe where he sat with his friend sipping hot tea. He gazed into the flickering flames before him.

"That's all true," he agreed. "But there's something about it that interests me. I'd like to be able to handle those challenges. I think I'd be stronger for it."

And so George volunteered to take the message, in spite of, or maybe because of, the hardships and dangers. Unfortunately, the French would not agree to what the British wanted. It wasn't long before the two powers were at war with each other. During this war George fought on the British side. Although there were many British successes, they also suffered some losses. Years later George was to remember and be grateful for these losses. When he returned home from this war, however, he was a young and famous soldier.

George always liked being close to nature, and after the war he wanted to settle down. He married Martha Custus, a young widow with two children, and they moved to Mount Vernon, a huge, beautiful plantation on the shore of the Potomac River. He became a lawmaker in the Virginia legislature. Many of the legislators made long speeches and tried to pass laws that would benefit themselves more than others. Not George though. His attitude would not let him do that. Instead, he made only a few speeches,

the ones he thought were important and necessary. And he listened, watched, and learned how a government works. For sixteen years he was a farmer, a landowner, and a businessman.

THINK ABOUT IT

1. What was George's attitude about working on the plantation when he was a young boy?
2. Tell about a time when George performed a dangerous mission for the British.

THE STRUGGLE FOR FREEDOM

After many peaceful years things suddenly began to happen between the Americans and the British. The British still thought of Americans as British— only not quite as good. At the same time the Americans were beginning to think of themselves as Americans, separate from the British. They began to want a government of their own. Some of the American leaders met in a congress to discuss the problems. They really wanted to avoid war, but no one was able to find a peaceful way to establish a government.

John Adams, from Massachusetts, who later became the second President of the United States, finally said: "Gentlemen, if we are going to have an army, we need a man to serve as Commander-in-chief."

Another delegate said, "I believe someone should be chosen from the Northern states, where most of our people live."

John Adams replied, "Sir, I disagree. George Washington is at present our most famous soldier and a man of great ability in the field. He is well-known for his courage and his ability to lead men. He is a man who could unite the colonies, and we will sorely need to be united for the task that lies ahead. Gentlemen, I nominate George Washington for the post of our commander-in-chief!"

What was George's attitude when he heard what these men wanted him to do? He knew they were asking him to do one of the hardest things he would ever have to do in his life. He knew there was hardly any army to command! Not only were there few men, but they were untrained as well. Also, there was no way to provide them with food, clothes, or ammunition. Most of them wanted to leave the army and go home, and many did.

This British army was large, expertly drilled, well-fed, and well-clothed. The Americans' shortages presented problems that would be difficult to solve, and yet George would have to solve them. He had served long and well already. He hadn't asked for this position. He was needed at home to run his affairs. Yet again, because of his attitude, George chose the biggest challenge, the way that would benefit the most people. These men, his friends, trusted him and believed he could lead them in their brave war for independence.

George told the Congress, "I beg it may be remembered by every person in this room that I this day declare with the utmost sincerity, I do not think myself equal to the command I am honored with." But he said, "yes." He was willing to try!

The struggle was hard, as he knew it would be. Yet, with his positive attitude, George was able to meet each problem with patience. He tried to do his best. He never had enough soldiers, and sometimes the ones he had were only there because they had been pushed out of their homes to fight.

Sometimes his men ran when they saw the British soldiers in their splendid, red-coated uniforms. You could not really blame them, for they were not trained. Some didn't want to be fighting the British anyway.

Many of the American soldiers didn't yet understand that they were fighting for freedom and a new country. It was Washington's job to train and inspire them. In order to help his men, George wrote many messages to Congress pleading for supplies, clothing, and food. The Congress wanted to help but wasn't sure how to go about equipping an army. Everyone was still new at building a country. So George's small army of soldiers suffered greatly, and its commander-in-chief suffered, too.

One of the worst times for George and his army happened during the winter of 1777-78 at Valley Forge, Pennsylvania. This is one of the most famous incidents in American history. Paintings, articles, books, and plays have been produced describing what happened at Valley Forge.

An aide to General Washington spoke to him. "General, we've lost the last two battles and now winter is coming fast. Where will we go?"

General Washington replied, "I intend to lead the troops to Valley Forge. We'll stay the winter there."

"Sir," the aide said, "pardon me, but that is hard country. The people there

are not sympathetic to the American cause. We can expect no food or shelter from them. It will be a difficult place to spend the winter."

"We have no choice," the general answered. "The British block our way. At least we will be safe there. For the rest we shall have to bear whatever fate may provide."

The soldiers built crude log huts for shelter, but the icy wind and snow blew in through cracks between the logs.

General Washington's aide spoke to him again. "General, the men are starving. They've long since worn their clothes to rags."

"That is true," General Washington replied. "I have seen our barefoot soldiers churning the deep snow while they scour the countryside seeking food. I see all this, and I hear their talk—the talk of desperate men. May the Lord give us the strength to bear what we have to bear. And may we find some good in all of this."

Washington's attitude helped him to try to find some good in a bad situation. When he tried to do that, it worked. A Prussian officer named Baron von Steuben arrived to help drill and train the soldiers. The baron worked the soldiers like they had never been worked before. In the spring General Washington said, "Now my army is trained and ready to fight."

Throughout the war Washington kept reminding himself of the lesson he had learned so long ago—that the British army could be beaten. He waited and watched, carefully planning his chance. Before long Washington's army found itself able to surround the main British army under Lord Cornwallis.

The British could not escape by sea, for the French had entered the war on the American side and the French navy blocked the harbors. Lord Cornwallis was forced to surrender his army to Washington. It was a great victory! How could the outnumbered army of General Washington possibly have caused the surrender of the magificent British troops? How had General Washington accomplished the impossible? When he was asked the question, Washington replied, "Only because God was on our side."

Now fifty-one, Washington had earned a good rest, and for that he gratefully returned to his beloved farm in Virginia. At Mount Vernon he once more took up the task of developing new and better ways of doing things on a farm.

As a young man Washington had stood in the woods facing the West, full of wonder about the great country that lay beyond. Now, as a man, he knew that country would one day develop into towns and farms. He knew

that people of this new country would settle there and even beyond, as far as the land went. He bought land whenever he could, and one time he rode 680 miles by horseback to be sure that his land was good.

Presently the leaders from the thirteen states met once again to form an American government. Washington met with them. His experience, ideas, and wisdom were too valuable to let him stay at home. This important meeting was called the "Constitutional Convention," and Washington was elected president of this convention. Once again he did not talk much but listened carefully to everything everybody else had to say. That was a lot of listening because each person felt the government should mean something special for his own state or part of the country.

Each of the delegates wanted to be sure the rights of his area would be protected.

"Our states are smaller in size than those in the West," reminded a man from the North.

"We are as yet undeveloped," spoke up a man from the West. "All the manufacturing and business go to the Northern states. Don't forget us!"

The delegate from the South was concerned about another issue. "Our plantations and our very way of life are different from the rest of the states," he said. "We must have the freedom to live as we choose!"

From the Western delegate came, "The Northern states have many more people than we do, but we still have a voice to be heard!"

Very few men at the convention understood that their central problem was to unite all the separate states into a single nation. Washington was one of the few who understood this. Even as a boy he had always looked beyond the horizon, and now he knew what it was he had envisioned: a country, grand and glorious almost beyond belief.

It would be vast, with deserts, mountains, valleys, and lakes that no one had yet seen, nor would see, in his lifetime. But it was there. He knew it was there. And the people who came to live in that vast land would have to be strong enough, wise enough, and unselfish enough to work for the good of the future. They would have to be willing to let their government take charge of things that would be for the betterment of the majority.

George listened to the arguments at the Constitutional Convention.

"I don't see why some of the delegates have to be so loud and angry," he said to a friend. "This is an important matter, and it deserves time and careful thought, not impatience and temper."

Eventually the United States Constitution was produced from this meeting of delegates. (The United States Constitution is a document which describes how our country is to be governed.) When enough states had approved the Constitution, the government was organized, and Washington was elected the first President of the United States.

"Congratulations!" cried his friend Jeff, giving George a sound slap on the back. "There couldn't be a better man for the job!"

George smiled, but his face had a serious look to it. "It is true that I like a challenge," he said. "But this task frankly overwhelms me. I do not have an example to look to because there has not been another president of this country. In fact," and a smile crossed his eyes, "there has not been a United States before!"

Now many of us wouldn't have responded with the courage and good will that George did. He could have refused the job and stayed at home, living a quiet and pleasant life. But his attitude made him willing to try, and when he tried, he always tried his best.

Washington was such a good president the first four years that he was elected president for another four years. At the end of his second term he wrote his famous Farewell Address, which was his final advice to the country.

Washington went home to Mount Vernon once more and looked after his land, took trips to watch the building of the new capital of the United States (called Federal City), and kept in touch with how things were going with the new government by writing many letters to friends.

THINK ABOUT IT

1. What kinds of problems faced George when he became commander-in-chief of the new American army?
2. What is an attitude?

A NATION SAYS FAREWELL

The last time I saw George out riding his horse was a snowy, cold day when he was sixty-seven. The wind and sleet were blowing into his face, and he got chilled. When he got back to Mount Vernon, he didn't change into warm, dry clothes like he should have. Instead, he did some paperwork while he was still dressed in his damp clothes. In the night he woke up with a severe sore throat. The doctors came and tried to help him, but there was nothing they could do. The next morning George Washington died.

It was almost impossible for Americans to believe the father of their country was no longer with them. Washington had led the country through hard times, suffered through Valley Forge, and helped to mold the character of a new nation.

Washington was loved and admired by a great many people, and they

wanted to honor his memory. The capital of the United States, Washington, D.C., was named for him. The Washington Monument was built in the capital, and the state of Washington was named for him. Cities, lakes, and schools throughout America were named after him, and his picture was put on our five cent postage stamp and on the one dollar bill.

So it was that the boy I watched become a man came to his final rest. I've always been proud of George and the way he played his part in turning the dream of a new nation into reality. I know he'd be pleased if you could find something in his example that would help you be a better person. He

believed in being happy with his family, friends, and neighbors. He set his mind to overcoming challenges and became a stronger person for having done it. If you could find a way to help your country stay strong and free, that would please him.

Sometimes when I'm flying over Mount Vernon, I can almost hear the sound of George's favorite horse galloping over the ridges and through the woods. The smell of magnolia blossoms makes the Virginia air seem sweeter

and finer than any on earth. I remember how much George loved this land and how everything he ever did proved that love. He had a wonderful attitude toward life.

Well, it's time for me to be on my way. You've seen some of the great moments in Washington's life, now go and make some of your own. Good luck, and I'll be watching to see what kind of attitude you decide to have!